WHAT WE CAN DO ABOUT

LITTER

Donna Bailey

Franklin Watts

New York   London   Toronto   Sydney

Franklin Watts
387 Park Avenue South
New York, NY 10016

Design: Julian Holland Publishing Ltd.
Picture Research: Alison Renwick
Printed in Italy

Library of Congress Cataloging-in-Publication Data
Bailey, Donna.
  Litter/Donna Bailey.
    p.   cm. – (What we can do about)
  Includes index.
  Summary: Describes how litter is a threat to many communities,
and provides suggestions for recycling and cleanup activities.
  ISBN 0-531-11016-8
  1. Litter (Trash) – Juvenile literature. 2. Refuse and refuse
disposal – Juvenile literature. [1. Litter (Trash) 2. Refuse and
refuse disposal.] I. Title. II. Series.
TD813.B35   1991
363.72'88 – dc20   90-45006
                                                    CIP   AC

Photograph acknowledgements

t = top b = bottom

Cover: Adrian Neville/Robert Harding Picture
Library, pp 6b Sally Neal/S & R Greenhill, 7t Robert
Arnold/Planet Earth Pictures, 7b Chris Fairclough
Colour Library, 8t Chris Fairclough Colour
Library, 9t N G Blake/Bruce Coleman Limited, 9b J
Allan Cash Photo Library, 10b Earl Young/Robert
Harding Picture Library, 11t Norman Owen
Tomain/Bruce Coleman Ltd, 11b Stephen Dalton/
NHPA, 12t John Birks/ICCE Photo Library, 12b P
A Hinchliffe/Bruce Coleman Limited, 13t Stephen
Krasemann/NHPA, 13b Jim Damaske/Planet
Earth Pictures, 14b J Tomkins/The Environmental
Picture Library, 15t Robert Harding Picture
Library, 15b Charlotte Macpherson/The
Environmental Picture Library, 16b G
Boutin/Robert Harding Picture Library, 17t Chris
Fairclough Colour Library, 17b The National Trust
Photographic Library, 18b M P Kahl/Bruce
Coleman Limited, 19t Jimmy Holmes/The
Environmental Picture Library, 19b Jen & Des
Bartlett/Bruce Coleman Limited, 20b D Christellis/
The Environmental Picture Library, 21 Jack
Dermid/Bruce Coleman Limited, 22b Chris
Fairclough Colour Library, 23t Chris Fairclough
Colour Library, 23b S & R Greenhill, 24b
Norreboom/Greenpeace Communications Limited,
25b Chris Fairclough Colour Library, 26b Chris
Fairclough Colour Library, 27b Chris Fairclough
Colour Library.

Contents

What is litter?

If you drop a candy wrapper or an empty potato chip bag in the street, you create litter. People who throw trash out of their car windows or leave **garbage** on the beach after a picnic also create litter. Litter is trash that has been dropped carelessly, or has not been collected and put in a garbage can.

Paper, plastic bags, glass bottles, metal cans and scraps of food can all become litter if they are not put in the right place when they are finished with. Things like glass bottles that can be **recycled** should be saved. They can be returned to the grocery store or put in a **recycling bin**. Other garbage should be placed in a trash can or taken home to put in your own garbage can.

Litter makes our towns, countryside and beaches look messy. Many people do not seem to notice litter. They do not see the pieces of plastic on lawns, fences and along roadsides. They do not think about the bottles and soda cans in the ditches. They do not notice the scraps of paper blowing around our city streets and pavements.

Who creates litter?

No one likes friends and visitors to drop pieces of paper, banana peels and soda cans in their homes. Many people, however, happily drop their trash at football games and in other public places. These people forget or do not care that someone else will have to clean up their garbage. How would you feel if you had to pick up all the trash in the picture?

Sometimes people are too lazy to clean up after themselves. It is so much easier to leave the remains of a picnic on the ground than to carefully pick up the pieces and take them home. People do not stop to think that the litter they leave behind them spoils the **scenery** for other people.

Some people dump old furniture and other unwanted things on country roads, in vacant lots, in pits and in rivers. This is called **illegal dumping**.

Businesses, such as building and hauling firms, also create a lot of litter. Broken bricks, old bits of wood and plastic tubing are often left behind on building sites. Trash of all kinds gets blown off uncovered trucks and is left to litter the roadside.

Litter in the town

Large numbers of people live and work in
towns and cities and they create a lot of litter.
People drop cigarette butts and empty cigarette
packs on the pavements and in gutters. They do
not think of the mess they are making.

Lots of people enjoy a quick snack of burgers and fries, but afterward they just drop the containers on the ground. Fast-food restaurants are often surrounded by piles of **discarded** containers.

A town soon begins to look scruffy and dirty if there are piles of litter in the streets. Nobody enjoys shopping in such dirty places.

Restaurants and stores often leave garbage in untidy piles outside their doors. Animals, such as cats, dogs, raccoons, and possums, knock over garbage cans to look for food, and trash gets spread over the pavement.

Litter with food in it is a **health hazard** in towns. The food attracts rats, mice and flies. These creatures carry diseases which can be passed on to people.

Litter in the countryside

People who visit the countryside, such as picnickers, are not always careful to take their trash home with them. Other litter in the countryside is created by the people who live there. Some farmers leave old machinery to rust in the corners of fields. They may also leave cans that have held dangerous **chemicals** lying around.

Litter in the countryside harms wildlife. Animals get caught in coils of rusty wire. When they get caught inside plastic bags, they are unable to breathe and they die. Animals can be **poisoned** by carelessly discarded cans that held paint and chemicals.

Every year, thousands of small animals die when they get trapped in bottles and cans. Tiny field mice slip into bottles to look for food. They cannot get out again up the slippery sides so they starve to death.

Litter thrown into rivers and lakes is just as dangerous. Discarded plastic circles that hold soda cans together are very difficult to see in water. Fish get trapped in the holes and cannot escape.

Garbage also blocks streams so that the water cannot flow. The still water soon gets choked by weeds. Fish and most water insects cannot live in these conditions.

Many wild duck and geese die because careless fishermen leave bits of fishing tackle in the water. Nylon fishing lines get wound around the ducks' beaks and hooks get caught in their throats. The birds are then unable to feed and starve to death.

This pelican has part of a fishing line wrapped around its wing.

Litter on the beach

Most of the litter we see on the beach has been washed ashore from ships that have dumped their garbage overboard. Some of this garbage sinks to the bottom of the sea, and some is broken down into small harmless pieces by the water. Glass bottles and most plastics do not break down, or **biodegrade**, for a long time and may be washed around the oceans for many years.

Vacationers often leave litter on the beach. In many countries, the beaches are swept clean every day. The picture shows beach cleaners in Rio de Janeiro, Brazil, collecting discarded garbage.

Litter on beaches can hurt people. If you leave broken glass or sharp metal ring-pulls from soda cans on the beach, they can easily get buried in the sand. Other people can then get nasty cuts on their feet from this litter.

Clearing up the mess

When litter has been dropped, we have to pay someone to pick it up. Your local city or town council makes sure the streets are cleaned. They pay people to empty garbage cans into large trucks. In most cities, road cleaners regularly clean the pavements. Machines with rotating brushes sweep the streets clean of litter every night.

In the countryside and on the beaches it is more difficult to use machines to clear away litter. In popular recreation spots, people have to be paid to pick up the litter left by visitors. Sometimes they use a long stick, called a **pick stick**. The stick means that the cleaners do not have to bend over or use their hands to pick up the litter.

Voluntary groups, such as **conservation** organizations, often ask people to help in cleaning up places that are badly polluted with litter. The young people in the picture are helping to clean out a river for a conservation group. When the river is clean, the water will be able to flow freely again. Fish and water plants will be able to live in the river once more.

Telling people about litter

Sometimes people do not realize that their litter can be dangerous to other people and animals, as well as looking messy and ugly.

The seal in the picture will die unless it can free itself from the fishing net.

All over the world there are groups that have been set up to tell people about the problems that litter can cause. These groups produce posters and other **publicity material** to try to persuade people not to drop litter.

People are most likely to remember not to drop litter if a poster has a good, clear message.

Nature reserves and national parks put up notices to remind visitors that litter can harm wildlife. This notice in a national park in Africa reminds travelers that they should only leave vehicle tracks when they cross the desert.

Rules about litter

Most countries have rules or laws against littering. In some places, people who are caught dropping litter in the street have to pay a **fine** on the spot. Can you find out what the fines are for dropping litter, or for dumping garbage, where you live?

There are also laws in some countries that make people clean up litter that has been dropped. In Switzerland, people who work in stores must sweep the street in front of their store every morning.

If people get money back when they return bottles and cans, they are less likely to drop them as litter. In Sweden, people pay a **deposit** on cans of soft drinks and beer. They can put the empty cans into a **reverse vending machine** and get a coin back in exchange. The cans will then be recycled.

In the United States, some people collect all their cans then sell them to a buyer who calls regularly at a local shopping center.

It's up to you!

You can do a lot to prevent litter. First of all, remember the rule: **LEAVE NO LITTER.** Put your garbage in a can if there is one. If not, or if the can is full, take your litter home. Tell your local authorities if the bin is never emptied. Put fast-food containers into the trash cans provided at the restaurants.

Remember that a diet of potato chip bags and scraps of unwanted food is not good for wild animals. The wrong food can make them ill, so put your garbage in the trash can after a picnic.

You should tell the police if someone is dumping garbage in the wrong place. Sometimes envelopes with addresses are found in the dumped garbage. The addresses may help the police to catch the person who did the dumping.

Many of the goods we buy are wrapped several times. Bags of chips come packed within larger cellophane wrappers and fruit is often put on trays covered in plastic. To help reduce garbage and litter, do not buy things that have more wrapping than is really needed.

There are other ways in which you can avoid creating garbage in the first place. Make sure you take your own bag with you when your family goes shopping, and do not accept plastic bags handed out free in supermarkets. Most stores will not insist that your purchase be wrapped in a bag, as long as you keep your receipt. If you have forgotten a bag, supermarkets often have cardboard boxes you can put your groceries in.

Cleanup

As well as making less litter yourself, you can encourage other people to do something about litter. Tell your family and friends about the problems litter causes. You could try to persuade your family to pick up litter from your yard, the street outside your home or the beach.

Perhaps you and your friends could run a cleanup **campaign** on the school grounds. Ask your teacher to help you organize this. Your teacher may also be willing to spend class time discussing what can be done about litter.

Another idea for you and your friends is to **"adopt"** a place, such as a local phone booth or bus stop. Visit it regularly to pick up any litter and make sure your adopted place is kept clean and tidy. If you want to "adopt" somewhere bigger, like a whole neighborhood or street, it might be a good idea to hold a "litter day" to get the area cleaned up. You will need to persuade lots of people to come along. Make sure you have collected a good supply of big plastic bags for the garbage. Ask an adult to take the bags to a legal garbage dump at the end of the day.

Be safe!

Although cleaning up litter with your friends can be fun, you must be careful.

Follow these rules.

1 Ask at least one adult to help you.

2 Make sure you have a first-aid kit handy in case anyone gets hurt.

3 Wear old clothes; your good clothes may get dirty or torn.

4 Wear rubber or plastic gloves when you pick up cans, bottles and food litter.

5 When possible, use a pointed stick to pick up paper trash.

6 Ask an adult to handle any broken glass you find.

7 Tell the police if you find dangerous things, such as containers with chemicals in them or **medical supplies**. DO NOT TOUCH THEM YOURSELF.

8 Do not eat while you are collecting the garbage, and wash your hands very well when you have finished.

Activities

1 Why not ask your teacher to help you organize an antilitter campaign? Your local conservation group may want to join in too.

You could design an antilitter poster, and give an antilitter button to the person who has picked up the most litter.

2 Make a survey of the municipal waste cans in your area. Are they all the same size and shape? Are there enough of them? Check how often they are emptied. If you think there should be more cans, write to your local authorities with the results of your survey.

Glossary

adopt: to agree to look after something.

biodegrade: to rot or to be broken down naturally by bacteria.

campaign: an event or events organized to get something done.

chemical: any substance which can change when joined or mixed with another substance.

conservation: the caring for and protection of something, especially wildlife and nature.

deposit: a small amount of money paid on something. The money is returned later if, for example, the bottle or container is returned to the store.

discard: to throw away something thought useless.

fine: to make someone pay a sum of money when he or she has done something wrong.

garbage: something that is no longer wanted.

health hazard: something that may be dangerous to people's health.

illegal dumping: throwing away large unwanted items of garbage in the wrong place.

infection: something that causes disease and illness.

medical supplies: things used to help treat people who are ill, such as bottles of pills or needles for injections.

pick stick: a long, pointed stick which is poked through litter to pick it up.

poison: a substance which harms or kills a person, plant or animal.

publicity material: posters, leaflets, buttons and other things produced to tell people a certain message.

recycle: to process something in order to regain the material for human use.

recycling bin: a bin where people can leave empty glass bottles so that the glass can be collected and used again.

reverse vending machine: a machine that will give back the deposit paid on a container when the bottle or can is placed inside it.

scenery: a view or landscape.

suffocate: to stop the breathing of a living thing.

voluntary: things done without payment.

Index